# Voices of Hope

## E STORIES OF RESILIENCE, RECOVERY, AND RENEWAL

Edited by Edward McCann

READ650 • 1 WRITER. 5 MINUTES. 650 WORDS.

Founder / Editor • Edward McCann
Executive Producer • Richard Kollath
Senior Editor / Literary Ombudsman • Steven Lewis
Senior Editor • David Masello
Editor • Karen Dukess
Editor • Lisa Donati Mayer
Design Director • Diane Fokas
Director of Photography • Kevin O'Connor
Chief Audio Engineer • Jesse Chason
Copy Editor • Shelley Sadler Kenney
Marketing Consultant • Jane Kaupp
Technical Advisor • Conrad Trautmann


**Advisory Committee**
Art Bell, Sara Caldwell, Richard Kollath, Ann Levin, Steven Lewis
David Masello, Irene O'Garden, John Pielmeier, Susan Ragusa
Andi Rosenthal, James Russek, Angela Derecas Taylor

"Do not judge me by my success, judge me by how many times
I fell down and got back up again." —*Nelson Mandela*

How do you get to Carnegie Hall? The answer to this old joke is as apt for the writer as it is for the musician: both need to practice, practice, practice.

Carnegie Hall's mission to present extraordinary music and musicians aligns with our efforts to promote excellent writers and writing, and so the invitation to partner in Carnegie Hall's *Voices of Hope* festival was music to our ears. As you'll see in these pages, it was also an opportunity for our writers to mine their own experiences, crafting personal narratives of creativity and resilience in the face of trying circumstances. These stories stand as a testament to the human spirit—examples of hope itself given voice.

Read650 is a literary nonprofit promoting writers through live and digital performances that celebrate the spoken word—a forum organized around single, broad topics featuring 650-word personal stories that can be performed in five minutes. The recorded performances from our events are added to a growing archive of writers reading their work aloud, with additional exposure through podcasts, broadcasts, our YouTube channel, and in printed volumes like the one you hold in your hand.

At Read650 we showcase writers of all ages with good stories to tell, with first-timers sometimers sharing the bill with bestselling authors. That's because it's all about the writing—word choices, the arc of a narrative, and the poetry of a unique literary voice. To submit your work or attend our shows, visit our website or Facebook page, and join our mailing list. Tell your writer friends about us, and please help spread the word about the spoken word.

*Ed McCann*

Edward McCann, Founder / Editor

READ650.ORG
FACEBOOK.COM/READ650

# CONTENTS

# CONTENTS

# Voices of Hope

JE STORIES OF RESILIENCE, RECOVERY, AND RENEWAL

# DEBORAH BATTERMAN

**Deborah Batterman** is the author of *Just Like February*, a finalist in the 2019 Next Generation Indie Book Awards, and the 2018 Best Book Awards, International Fiction Awards, and American Fiction Awards. A story from her collection, *Shoes Hair Nails*, was nominated for a 2006 Pushcart Prize and her award-winning stories and essays have appeared in anthologies as well as print and online literary journals. A native New Yorker, she has worked over the years as a writer, editor, and teaching artist. Her blog, *All the Small Things*, is an exploration of all the small things, and the big ones, that impact our day-to-day lives.

# THE HALF-FULL / HALF-EMPTY CUP

Deborah Batterman

It was forty-two degrees the other day, the sun deciding to show itself after a spell of grey and very cold February days. Today the lake is frozen enough for ice skaters. Spring is just around the corner.

I got my first COVID vaccine dose last week, which renders a sense of renewal as personal as it is seasonal. My daughter, three thousand miles away, texts me: halfway toward no more COVID phobia!

And yet . . .

There's something surreal, after all the months spent sheltering in place—worrying and stocking up, trying to work—about sitting in a roomful of people at individual stations where nurses inject needles into our arms, and we wait the prescribed fifteen minutes to be sure of no serious adverse reaction.

I scan the room, start to see a new story waiting to take shape. An unmasked weariness shows itself in the eyes of the woman across from me. I intuit a complicit smile in the masked half of her face. Relief? Uncertainty? Seems like ages ago since daily focused writing gave a familiar, needed rhythm to my day. Now that I'm just picking up where I left off, it seems like only yesterday. Pandemic time is a world unto itself.

In normal times, making sense of the world, through essays and fiction, gives purpose to my days. Yet the double whammy of a psychopath-in-chief and a pandemic pushed me into a state of anxious despair. It became too easy to be distracted, restless. At best, I would write in fits and starts.

Nevertheless, I persisted. I would continue blogging, finding myself in a chorus of writers bonded by hashtags—#mycoronadiaries #pandemic2020—until I couldn't. A period of retreat set in.

Toni Morrison's thoughts about being too depressed to write following the election of George W. Bush in 2004 resonated deeply.

"I can't seem to work, to write," she recalls saying to a friend. "It's as though I am paralyzed, unable to write anything more in the novel I've begun. I've never felt this way before, but the election…." Her friend's response is a resounding "No! No, no, no! This is precisely the time when artists go to work—not when everything is fine, but in times of dread. That's our job."

And yet, getting to work requires more than an act of will. It requires a receptive mind that sees the half-full cup as also half-empty and an open heart that knows it's in the emptiness where possibility thrives.

Leonard Cohen said it best.

"There is a crack in everything/that's how the light gets in."

I look for the light day after day. I find new things to cook, a tangible alternative for the creative impulse that, in less fraught times, drives my need to write. I go for walks. I listen to music.

Rachmaninoff wrote his Piano Concerto No. 2 following a period of despair. The negative response to his Symphony No. 1 left him unable to compose for three years. I knew none of this the first, second, third, tenth time I listened to the piece, always brought to tears by the music.

I listen to myself, hear rumblings of the unsettling rhythm pandemic life has brought to my days. A visceral restlessness has me obsessed with divesting things that no longer serve me well, reorganizing closets and drawers, asking myself why didn't I do this before?

No one would choose a pandemic to force their hand at anything, but the ripple effect of restlessness takes me off auto-pilot and to a deeper solitude that has me seeing everything I do in a new light.

With fresh eyes I return to an unfinished collection, a bit more settled enough to transmute the tangle of real-life love and loss and grief and anger, sown from a time like no other, into tales that turn tears into tropes.

# ELIZABETH BAYOU-GRACE

**Elizabeth Bayou-Grace** lives in Western Massachusetts with her husband and their cat and dog. She received her BA from Warren Wilson College and her MFA from Texas State University and her writing has been published in *Sixfold*. She has performed her poetry at the Poetry at Roundtop, ArtOutside in Rockdale, Texas, and the Wakarusa Music Festival and Camping Festival.

# HOPE

Elizabeth Bayou-Grace

Recently, I was gathering myself together to write a poem that I knew would be difficult, both in terms of craft and terms of heart, and I was really taking my time about it. I was just standing there in the doorway of the living room, scanning the room for any possible thing I might need in the next few hours: tea, a blanket, snacks, an extra book, inhaler, laptop, headphones, candle, maybe a totem, maybe something to fidget with. Finally, I resigned to the need and wished my husband goodbye. He responded with, "have fun."

Have fun? I was going into battle. I was entering a room where only I live. I was going to wrestle a monster who speaks in riddles. I was going to cry and bleed and grow a new grey hair. It was most assuredly not going to be a fun time. Most times, I would rather do anything than write. I find it painful and difficult, and yet, I must. This may seem like an odd scene to center a piece about hope and healing, but by grounding the conversation here, I hope to remind myself that healing isn't always beautiful, and rarely is it fun, and yet, I must.

It's a lesson I need constant reteaching of, that hope can be ugly and chaotic. I learn it over and over again. This particular poem I was working on was meditating on the enormous loss we have collectively experienced in relation to Covid-19. That morning, we had officially lost 500,000 Americans. We have lost our heroes, our families, our friends, our stability. We have lost our rituals. I think this an especially important loss, and one we underestimate. The rules that previously kept us safe, no longer serve us.

Art is a product of the world in which it's created. I think of how paintings changed after World War I, how abstract they became. How poetry broke out of forms. Some of my favorite writers were working in those early post-WW-1 years, and I studied their brave leaps and their experiments. I often thought to myself how they were the pioneers in this wild west of expression, how they still had humanity and art to explore, to see for the very first time. In today's world of unlimited access to texts, to the internet, to living voices in other countries, I thought it was impossible to discover something new for myself, to be truly experimental.

At some point during my MFA, with so many options as to how to write poetry, so many examples, so many voices, so many movements, I suddenly could no longer figure out how to break lines. What had once been somewhat intuitive now was cumbersome and artificial. I eventually found my way to formal poetry, as a way to at least prescribe myself some rules on line breaks. For years, I counted every single syllable I penned. And for years, those rules kept me safe and served my work.

When we entered our first lockdown, and many days since, writing has felt impossible. I did not know how to keep writing the same poems I had been, in a world that operated so differently. I couldn't. And suddenly, my poems broke open. They couldn't fit in forms. They got longer. In order to do the work of documenting this shift in history, I had to let go. I had to learn a new way to write poems. I had to mourn the loss of my old rituals. I had to build new rituals that failed.

It's been ugly at times. Chaotic, often. And some days, at the end of battle, I walk out of my office, limping but still triumphant. Today, wrestling with the monster didn't kill me. Today, I wrote a poem.

## KATHLEEN DONOHOE

**Kathleen Donohoe** is the author of two novels published by Houghton Mifflin Harcourt, *Ashes of Fiery Weather* (2016) and *Ghosts of the Missing* (2020). Her short fiction has appeared in several literary magazines including *Conjunctions, Washington Square Review,* and *Harpur Palate.* She was raised in Brooklyn, New York, where she still lives with her husband and son.

# NAME THE GHOSTS

Kathleen Donohoe

I parted the blue curtain of the lone window. The siren, though, grew fainter as the ambulance carried its scream down another Brooklyn block, away from my apartment. The avenue below used to be busy even at midnight. But now, the bus stop, the crosswalk, the gas station on the corner were deserted, and the scene below looked like a Hopper painting where all the people have gotten up and walked away.

It was April 2020 and New York's Covid numbers were still in their vertiginous climb. My husband and son were asleep, so I was alone in what we call our living room, though we don't own a couch. It's furnished with a bookcase, a desk and a wooden table we snagged off a curb in Park Slope and hauled home on the F train. That table is where I was sitting, hopscotching through time.

I was logged into Ancestry.com and my laptop screen was full of pink and blue squares, connected each to each by black lines, a network of family. With one click, I was in Depression-era Brooklyn; another, in 1920s rural Ireland; then it was 1860 and I was in Five Points, Manhattan's most notorious slum.

My second novel came out two months ago. I had started a new book and I was supposed to be working on it. I'd stayed up late to write. A paragraph. A page. A single sentence. Getting started is always like trying to fly without a set of wings. In quarantine, it felt like attempting flight without a sky.

Every day, as I worked at my administrative assistant job and homeschooled, intrigued by fourth grade history but stumped by the math, I did so through a pressing panic that a family member would get sick and also, conversely, that I, at least, would not. When the world rejoined, I wondered how I would face the survivors, the grieving, the health care workers. To say that during the pandemic I wrote would never be enough.

Scanning the names of my family arrayed in front of me, I realized I was in the upper reaches of my tree, entirely in Ireland and solely among the dead. I'd read in some tweet that, during these difficult times, I should be journaling by hand, creating a record. I got up from the table and fetched the blank book I'd bought in early March and had barely used, unable to do even that consistently.

The leather cover was embossed with Celtic knot work. Picking up the pen I left tucked inside, I opened to a blank page and began to write names of ancestors whose stories I'd pieced together through historical records.

Brigid Keane of Ireland. My third great-grandmother gave birth nearly every year of the Great Hunger, which ravaged Ireland from 1847-1852.

Martin Walsh. My third great-grandfather came to New York from Ireland in 1847. In 1860, he was living with his wife, four children and his mother in Five Points, Manhattan. He died ten years later at the age of 48. I don't know how, not yet.

Lizzie Broderick. My second great-grandmother, born in Ireland, died of tuberculosis in a Brooklyn tenement on June 16, 1904.

Charles Brady. My great-granduncle died in New York City of chronic alcoholism in 1908. He was twenty-five.

Edward McNally. My great-uncle died of scarlet fever at the age of two in a Brooklyn tenement on March 17, 1913.

Flossie Ryan. My great-aunt died at twenty of phlebitis (some months) in Derrymullan, Galway, Ireland, 1922.

I set the pen down. My 1980s Catholic school penmanship lacked the artistry of the Census takers, but in looking at what I wrote, I felt a similar pull, a way to call across generations. I see you, or maybe, I remember. This is the work, to name the ghosts.

## LYNN EDELSON

**Lynn Edelson** has been writing memoir for the past ten years and is currently at work on a collection of short stories. In 2016, her essay, "Heart Monitor," was selected to be part of the NYC Listen To Your Mother show. Seven of her pieces have been published by Read650, included in the books, *What We Wore, My Library, Holidays, Back To High School, Summer Jobs, On Mothers,* and *VOICES OF HOPE.* Lynn is the mother of two grown sons, and lives in the Hudson Valley with her husband, Michael Principe and their two dogs.

# COUNTERPOINT

Lynn Edelson

"Here?" Arthur asks, pointing to an open space.

"Looks good," I say.

Our husbands nod in agreement as they drop the bags of food and sand-chairs to the grass. We set up our things, and even though the sun is in our eyes, we're happy to be finally sitting down. I place myself between Arthur and my husband and reach for the bag of chips.

Yo-Yo Ma is closing out the season at Tanglewood with The Bach Project, and the lawns are packed with the fifteen dollar ticket holders.

As the sun begins to set, the landscape darkens. Loud applause echoes as Yo-Yo walks out onto the empty stage, bows and smiles at us all. He sits down on the lone chair that stands behind the cello. A hush falls over the crowd, as his bow moves across the strings.

I am entranced. Bach is my go-to guy, the one who fill
me up when the days are longer and the nights are darker, when
the quiet echoes within. The mathematics are seductive; th
counterpoint melodies keep me spellbound. I reach for my hus
band's hand, because only he knows how joyful I am feeling.

It is not until the end of the fourth suite that Yo-Yo fi
nally speaks. He thanks us for being there, for supporting thi
international project to heal political divisiveness, for bearing
witness. Then he introduces the next suite.

"This one is especially meaningful for me," he tells us
"When I'm feeling depressed, or in need of renewal, this is th
piece I go to for solace. So, this is dedicated to all of those who
have experienced loss. The loss of health, of love, the loss o
dignity."

I am stunned by his words.

He is speaking directly to my heart. The heart that is try
ing to wrap itself around my son who is struggling to find hi
way as he moves past the life he shared with the woman he
loved. I am sitting in the dark thinking about my child, the on
who hears all the words not spoken, the one who cannot ye
envision a future without her by his side.

I am no longer holding my husband's hand. I am trying
to breathe into the night, holding on to the stars, holding on to
a whisper of hope.

Yo-Yo moves through the piece with tenderness and be
gins the final suite, but I can't keep up. I am still caught up i
his words, in the gentle nod of his head, until the music finally

stops, and he speaks to us again.

"Thank you thank you," he begins.

And then he talks about Tanglewood, about the impact it has had on the culture, and especially for the opportunities it provides young musical talent.

"And to that end," he says with a grin, "we found someone who wrote a wonderful song at the age of 20. May I introduce to you, Jimmy Taylor."

And out walks James Taylor onto the stage. The crowd gasps and then erupts in applause, and starts calling his name. He sits on a stool very close to Yo-Yo and they begin to play "Sweet Baby James." The audience begins cheering as Taylor is singing, until they finally settle into the music.

And me? I am weeping. My hands are in my lap, my fists are tight, and I am smiling as tears are streaming down my cheeks and all I can think about is magic.

This moment, the joy of this surprise.

I am sobbing silently into the darkness, even as everyone around me is laughing and singing along. And I am filled up with love and the hope that perhaps, just perhaps, those magical moments are still out there for my son. That they will come upon him when he's not looking, when he has given up, when he can no longer see the stars.

## JULIE EVANS

Pursuing a life-long mission to help people recover the health, humor, or peace of mind they may have lost along the way, **Julie Evans** uses her skills as a licensed massage therapist, ordained deacon, freelance writer, and motivational speaker to bring her unique healing skills to those around her. Julie's writing has appeared in Thrive Global, *Woodstock Times, Healthy Hudson Valley, Healthy You, Pulse, KevinMD,* and *Into Sanity.* She has read her work for NPR, Read650 and the Woodstock Story Slams. Woodstock Arts published her memoir, *Joy Road: My Journey from Addiction to Recovery* in 2019.

# BAPTIZING JOHN COLTRANE

Julie Evans

During the pandemic I set out to find a photograph of John Coltrane my husband had seen in a shop window. Our anniversary was in three weeks and I always give him gifts that honor his music because music saved his life. At fourteen he had picked up a clarinet and could play any song his mother selected; then he found the saxophone, and it didn't matter so much that he was a clumsy kid, bullied at school or had a father who beat him. Music became his safe place.

I found the photograph he'd seen but it wasn't for sale. I look online and find a photo of Coltrane as a young man holding onto his horn like it's part of him, just like I've seen Tommy do a thousand times. The seller wants $250. The picture is out of focus and I wish I could see it up close. I see a tab to contact the seller. I click on it asking if I can come see the photo. He texts back his address and off I go. My GPS takes me on a route I've never driven. I open the windows to let in the fresh spring air.

Magnolia trees in full bloom, the sky so blue, and the clouds wispy like feathers. I turn the final corner onto his street just as an old beat-up Jeep careens around the corner stopping right beside me.

He stretches out his massive hand to shake mine and tips his head in the direction of the driveway indicating I should follow him. He drives with his door open and foot hanging out. He's already striding up the porch stairs as I approach the house. I hurry to catch up but he stops me.

"Wait."

I only get a glimpse through the broken screen of a hallway crowded with every kind of thing. I back down the steps and stand next to a red hibiscus bush wondering how a tropical plant survives in upstate New York. I used to live in Jamaica where such plants were common as was the seller's thick accent.

"I love your plant." I say as he hands me the photograph.

The black and white photo is behind filthy glass inside a rusted metal frame. My eye is drawn to a blue ink spot on Coltrane's tweed jacket.

"I noticed that," he says reassuringly. "Just give me $200."

My eyes move from the photograph to the man's faded blue flip-flops, the big toenail so long it curls around the toe. I raise my eyes taking in the worn khaki pants cut off above the ankle, his thin white cotton shirt unbuttoned one too low. He slips his mask up from the tangle of his thick gray beard to cover his mouth. The wind stirs the blossoms on the hibiscus. I give him the $200. dollars. He doesn't offer me a glass of water or use of the bathroom. We touch elbows and I drive home.

Early the next day, I rush to Fredericka's framing studio. I hand her the photograph. She unscrews each tiny screw then gently pries the rusted frame loose and lifts the murky glass from the photograph. Coltrane's shoulders lift from the backing. His head moves from side to side like Stevie Wonder and then his chest pushes upward as if he is taking a breath. I watch as John Coltrane comes to life just like Tommy does every time he plays.

After ordering the frame all we can do is wait. Tragically, the next day George Floyd is murdered. Fredericka becomes absorbed with tending to John Coltrane's wounds. With a damp cloth she dabs at a spot on the photograph and surprised when it comes clean, she asks if I'm willing to let her submerge the whole thing in water, like a baptism. I say yes.

## SARAH FEARON

Native New Yorker **Sarah Fearon** is a graduate of The High School for the Performing Arts and New York University. She writes and performs both comedy or tragedy and says "sometimes it's the same thing." Just prior to the Covid pandemic, her one person show, *2B, A Bottomless Cup of Real Estate Crazy* ran at The Friars Club as well as the Players Theater in Greenwich Village. As a real estate salesperson, she spends much of her day doing laps around the city on foot or on a bicycle. Sarah serves on the board of Irish American Writers and Artists.

# FIND LOST FOUND

Sarah Fearon

Just before Valentine's Day 2020 and approaching almost a full year of heartache, I was walking from Central Park West on Seventy-sixth Street toward Columbus Avenue.

I was yakking on the phone with my friend Regina when I cut myself off: "Hold on, let me call you back. I just found a blue pouch on the ground. Let me try to work some good karma."

Without hesitation, Regina said, "Go get it, girl."

I picked up the pouch from the base of a tree, then pulled the drawstrings open. Knowing it must be an important treasure with sentimental value to someone, I peeked inside. Glanced again to get a glimpse of sparkle nestled in the periwinkle-meets-Tiffany blue sack: a bracelet of Greek evil eye beads strung together with alternating disks of faux diamonds.

I assumed whoever lost it must be upset. I looked at the closest brownstone door and wondered whether I should knock, or maybe just press all the buzzers.

I chose the buzz all method, and a few moments later some guy opened the inner glass door.

"I was passing by and I think someone lost this," I said. He was sweet but silent, and I became afraid that I may sound hoax-y, adding "If I make a sign do you have any tape?" He came back a few moments later with packing tape, and, in exchange, I gave him one of my holiday cards about clapping out of the windows at 7PM during COVID to prove I was well-intentioned.

I got the sign taped up: "found blue pouch...call this number."

Then, glancing back at the scene of the find, I noticed a Zappos box near the tree. Transported into the opening credits of my own episode of Law & Order, I flipped the box over as if it was a plastic forensic bag. The label had the exact address I was standing in front of—and someone's name. Maybe the pouch fell out of her pocket? I took a photo of the label and called the number. "Hello?" a woman answered.

"Hello, Angela? I was walking by and found a blue pouch and wonder if it might be yours."

"Yes," she said, "you are so nice to... I left it there on purpose, a few pieces of jewelry I did not want for someone to find."

I exhaled. "Oh. I thought it seemed important."

"That's so nice," she said.

I assured her I would find someone to give it to.

Then I took a picture of the treasures to show Regina: The evil eye bracelet plus another that had black beads with a silver arrow, a necklace with a bunny pendant, two mismatched earrings, and a salmon red woven string friendship bracelet with golden beads.

If I had decided to keep anything it would have been the friendship bracelet. Echoes of the call with the woman offered a renewed sense of the default human condition. A sudden awareness of the ramifications of the kindness of strangers … to strangers.

I decided then that I had to see the original intention to fruition and give it all away. But I also had to add something from me to manifest the gesture. So, I sewed the beads into the shape of a heart over the heart of a jacket, adding a few of my own colorful beads.

Keeping the friendship bracelet intact and tucked into the blue pouch, I placed the sack in the top pocket of my jacket. I imagined the heart of Greek eye beads would offer protection against any negative energy of the evil eye. I imagined looking into someone's eyes and handing it off. Then I left the embroidered jacket in a good spot for the treasure to be found.

# MIHAI GRÜNFELD

**Mihai Grünfeld** was born in Cluj, Romania where he lived until he was eighteen. In January 1969 he traveled to Czechoslovakia and from there escaped to the West. After a long journey he eventually settled in the United States. He obtained his PhD from University of California at Berkeley and has just retired from Vassar College where he taught Spanish and Latin American Literature. His autobiography, *Leaving – Memories of Romania*, was published in 2008. Together with Sarah Levine Simon he adapted his novel, *The Dressmaker's Secret*, into a play of the same name which enjoyed a successful one-month run in New York City.

# TRANSLATING MY UNCLE'S MEMOIR

Mihai Grünfeld

When I returned to Romania in 1993 to visit my Uncle Zoli, Ceausescu's hateful police regime had ended, and it was no longer dangerous for me to travel to the home I had escaped as a teenager.

I had always admired my uncle Zoli but knew little of his past other than he only completed elementary school; he was an intellectual, a man who read thousands of books, and the director of a factory in Bucharest. I was surprised when I gave him a whole-hearted hug and realized that he was shorter than me. His stodgy, solid body was still full of energy, but his face looked older and his eyes less vibrant. It was a warm June afternoon. His two-bedroom apartment was small and crowded. It had the feeling of an old man's place, so different from what I had remembered.

I placed my suitcase on the floor, and he led me into the tiny kitchen where from a gallon bottle he poured two half-glasses of his home-made, golden apricot brandy. We drank to our reunion.

That evening, after we got up from the abundant supper he had prepared, pork chops, French fries, and pickles, he signaled to me to come into the living room. "Leave those dishes," he said.

I sank in a deep soft couch and Zoli picked out a yellow manila envelope from one of the bookcases.

"This is for you," he said with a smile, as he pulled out a stack of handwritten pages. His hands were missing fingertips. They had scared me as a child, but I never had the courage to ask him what happened.

"What is this?" I asked. The manuscript had no cover, it was not stapled together, and its 105 pages were numbered and covered on both sides with a dense handwriting with beautifully curved letters, slightly tilted to the right. Written in Romanian.

"I wrote this for my grandchildren," Zoli said. "They should know what happened." He paused. "And you too should know. It is about four years of my life, first in the Jewish Labor Battalions on the Eastern Front and then as a prisoner in Auschwitz."

That evening I read the entire manuscript. I was not used to his handwriting and, impatient to find out what happened, I would read ahead, without always understanding. His story took me on a journey through the concentration camps where he had barely survived. It was personal and detailed, and although my parents never spoke about their experiences in Dachau and Auschwitz, I could easily imagine their horror through Zoli's words. It also explained his missing fingers, which had been amputated after he suffered frostbite in Ukraine.

Next morning, at the small kitchen table, Zoli served me the breakfast I had grown up on: a couple of slices of white bread with plum jam, and a cup of Nescafe. Sipping my coffee, I looked into his familiar blue eyes: "Why are you giving me this manuscript?"

"It's for you to do with whatever you want," he said softly. "If you could publish it, there in America, I'd like that. Here, people are not interested."

"I will have to translate it into English."

"Yes," he said. "You must do whatever is needed."

I have read Zoli's manuscript many times since that evening in 1993. It took me many years to be ready for the task of translating it into English. I had to first write my own memoir about growing up in Romania and escaping. I also needed to visit Auschwitz.

A year ago, my uncle's memoir was accepted for publication at Yad Vashem, the Jerusalem Holocaust Museum. I feel I have honored Zoli Bácsi's request, and also given voice to my parents' unspoken journeys, their survival, and their incredible spirit to start their lives again and build a new family.

# PAUL GRUSSENDORF

**Paul Grussendorf** is an attorney representing refugees and asylees worldwide and in immigration court. His legal memoir is, *My Trials: Inside America's Deportation Factories*. He also writes fiction under the byline Jonathan Worlde. Jonathan Worlde's mystery novel, *Latex Monkey with Banana*, was winner of the Hollywood Discovery Award with prize of one thousand dollars. Recent short fiction appears in The Raven Review, the 2020 anthology *Ghost Stories of Shepherdstown*, and in *Cirque Journal*. He is also a traditional country blues performer under the stage name Paul the Resonator, whose CD is *Soul of a Man*.

# THE BIRTH OF PAUL THE RESONATOR

Paul Grussendorf

I came to Salloum, Egypt, a Bedouin town on the Mediterranean, in July 2011 to work with the UN Refugee Agency. We interviewed African refugees from Darfur who had found shelter in the UN refugee camp on the border with Libya, seeking resettlement. They had earlier fled Darfur because of violent incursions into their pastoral homelands by the Arab Janjaweed, a militia who were killing and plundering in order to drive them out. I was the only American in an international team.

I brought a small classical guitar with me, occupying my free hours playing country blues for anyone who cared to have a listen. I shared a house with three UN officers, a Norwegian guy named Siegfried a Canadian, Mark; and a Syrian, Anas.

Every morning we drove the eight kilometers up the escarpment on the Egyptian-Libyan border to the camp. In the windblown, dusty setting the prefabricated metal interview huts suffered constant power blackouts, causing loss of air conditioning and current for our laptops. We were always sweaty and exhausted by the end of the day. I especially appreciated working with our African interpreters, benefiting from their knowledge of the culture and their empathy for the refugees. They translated much more than the various languages.

Siegfried scheduled a goodbye party and asked if I could please play guitar. At first I declined, knowing the small guitar, without amplification, wouldn't carry well in an open space with a lot of people talking and socializing. But Siegfried insisted.

The night of the party, I wait until everyone had gotten their food and the general commotion was a bit died down. Around a hundred people, including twenty African interpreters, are enjoying themselves in the pleasant warm air under a starlit sky. I take my position on the steps facing the courtyard. My friends, seated in a semicircle about twenty to thirty feet out from me, create a natural amphitheater. They're expecting a show, but I'm not a showman. I've never played for more than a handful of people. I start with a bouncy tune, "Payday," by Mississippi John Hurt, one of the first tunes I learned decades ago. I notice the applause is decidedly loudest from the interpreters who are watching me with radiant faces.

I shift gears, playing "Wabash Rag," an upbeat ragtime tune by Blind Blake. His jazzy, highly syncopated guitar stylings were unmatched in the twenties when he recorded for the so-called Race labels, and he is still considered the paragon of fingerstyle blues guitarists. After the first chorus several of the Africans leap to their feet, boogying right in front of me, with hands in the air, eyes wide, heads shaking, displaying intricate footwork. Our colleagues join them, clapping hands. With a big smile my German friend does her version of a cakewalk.

The look of delight on the dancers' faces inspires me. I keep the beat going, astonished at this spontaneous eruption of musical synergy. For a half hour we've got an African juke joint happening, people kicking up their feet, dancing away the day's tedium, punctuated with occasional Darfurian leaps-into-the-air with shouts of joy. I play songs of Blind Boy Fuller, Reverand Gary Davis, and Blind Lemon Jefferson. When I rev up the beat in the chorus of "Police Dog Blues," Abraham, a Darfurian interpreter cries, "Oh, Mr. Paul, that is the kind of music we like!"

And in that moment I've found my true mission, to carry the African American country blues back to Africa and around the world. What stage name? Since I specialize in resonator guitar and the swampy sounds of the Mississippi Delta, I christen myself Paul the Resonator, a play on the old gospel tune John the Revelator. I'm born again—a blues missionary. I have since played in many refugee camps and schools in Africa, always with gratitude to those African interpreters who that night showed me the way.

# KATHLEEN McKITTY HARRIS

**Kathleen McKitty Harris** is a fifth-generation native New Yorker whose work has appeared in *Longreads*, *CRAFT Literary*, *Creative Non-fiction*, *McSweeney's Quarterly Concern*, and *The Rumpus*, among others. Her essay, "A Timeline of Human Female Development," appears in the anthology *My Body, My Words* (2018). She has also performed as a storyteller on *The Moth* podcast and co-hosts the 'What's Your Story?' live-reading series in northern New Jersey, where she lives with her husband and two children.

# ZOOMING THROUGH IT

Kathleen McKitty Harris

It's hard to sit down and write on any given day, but even more so during a pandemic. Yet a string of nine numbers served as the key to unlocking that discipline for me, even during such difficult times. Those nine digits were a Zoom meeting code for an online writing group, one that somehow kept me at my keyboard each week and kept me working.

As the coronavirus began to run rampant throughout the world last March, upending routines, lives, families, workplaces and economies, a friend suggested that we form a weekly online writing group along with several of our literary comrades. We needed focus in the time of Covid, and we needed distraction for the very same reason. As the encroaching reality of isolation grew nearer, we realized that we needed to see each other's faces on the screen, even if for just an hour or two each week. Even more than creative output and word counts, we needed camaraderie and companionship.

The premise was this: we'd write four or five pages each week—an essay for one, perhaps, a monologue for another, the beginnings of a chapter in a novel for a third—and log on at noon every Thursday to Zoom to share our stories and offer constructive feedback. At each meeting, we signed on a few minutes early to kibbitz and check in with each other. We shared our home remedies for sleeplessness, our recipes for sourdough starters, and our worries and anxieties. We shared news about who had tested positive for Covid and who, miraculously, had not. We shook our heads in disgust about presidential tantrums and science deniers. We complained about our circumstances and limitations and cried openly about what—— or who—— we were missing most that week. At every meeting, there were nods of compassion and words of strength emanating from each digitized rectangle.

Then, we'd read our work. Week after week, anywhere from three to six women would show up with several written pages. When I look back on that now, I can appreciate how herculean that was. At the time, it felt like nothing more than a lifeline that each of us reached for, hand over hand, to get to the following week. Now, that effort feels miraculous.

The writing didn't have to be spectacular. First drafts undoubtedly aren't. What was astonishing was that it appeared at all. Each week, the automated Zoom doorbell would ring, and these ordinary, industrious women would show up, again and again.

There were times, of course, when we cancelled class. We nixed it on the day after Election Day, because everyone was still glued to news reports, unable to focus on much past Georgia and Pennsylvania's vote counts. We skipped most of January altogether, because of the three successive Wednesdays that brought us insurrection and impeachment and inauguration. We recently cancelled when one of our classmates got her second Covid vaccine shot and ran a fever. But we kept coming back.

At times we wrote about Covid, but more often than not, we wrote about other themes of loss—a sibling's death in a long-ago childhood, aging parents, abuse, estrangement. Like mystic moments of birth and death, this time, too, opened a holy portal, and we entered it together.

The nearness of the pandemic and the resulting vulnerability that bubbled up somehow enabled us to aim closer to the bone. Covid had left us with cracked-open chests and festering wounds. The terrible beauty of that rawness enabled us to produce some of our most moving and honest pages.

I don't know if the group will continue after the pandemic ends. What I do know is how grateful I am for the company of strong women during this strange, strange time, for their gifted words and their entirely human hearts, and all that they can impossibly hold.

# SALLY HOSKINS

**Sally G. Hoskins** is a retired college biology professor formerly employed at City College of the City University of New York. There, she developed the CREATE project, aimed at transforming the teaching and learning of biology through a focus on close reading of primary literature (peer-reviewed research reports) rather than textbooks. She also founded and conducted SHE, a women's vocal ensemble (1998-2005) that gave free concerts and raised funds for NYC-based charitable organizations. Her essays have appeared in the *New York Times, Newsweek,* and *Science,* as well as in anthologies from the Visible Ink project and Read650.

# NOT AS EXPECTED:
## HOW WRITING MY FIRST BOOK
## GOT ME THROUGH THE PANDEMIC

Sally Hoskins

As a biologist, my initial reaction to the pandemic was, "Science will get us out of this," followed closely by, "People will soon understand and respect laboratory research much more." I was half-right.

I'm a retired college professor, living in a tiny cottage in Putnam County, where, last summer, I coped by trying to grow flowers from seed, taking long walks, and catching up on sitcoms I missed during graduate school. In a June phone session with my long-time psychiatrist, I rambled—again—about "someday" compiling the essays I'd produced in recreational writing classes into a book. This time, she said, "Why not self-publish?"

Feeling unmoored that day, I heard the suggestion as a command. I dug into my files and unearthed drafts of some seventy essays marked up years ago by writing group classmates, then spent the summer rewriting fifty of them, appreciative of every praised turn of phrase, correction of misused semicolons, or marginal "LMAO."

By September, I had a complete draft of "the book," though I learned that, as with grant proposals for the National Science Foundation, you're not done when it's written. Grants need budget justifications, facilities statements, and biosketches. A self-published book involves decisions on issues I'd never considered: dimensions, fonts, drop caps, headers and paper stock. The only easy part was the title—Not as Expected— the box I'd checked on more than one Lands' End "Reason for Return" form. It was an all-purpose excuse for rejecting something without having to explain how your expectations misaligned with reality. The title essay focused on the year I became an instant single mother to my orphaned teenage niece. For her, it was time to rebel against nonexistent parents. I, in contrast, was thinking Daughter I Never Had, or at least Gilmore gal-pal. Hijinks ensued.

I chose a book publishing crew from Ohio since I'm originally a Midwesterner. Their guidance helped until we got to cover design--another Not as Expected experience. They proposed taking that chore off my hands—for $500. Uh, no. I would do my own cover. It looked easier than parenting. I plucked a pink zinnia I'd personally germinated, photographed it emerging from an eggshell, then mastered a minimal InDesign skillset. Even though it took me half a day to figure out how to draw a frame around the photo, doing everything myself was undeniably satisfying.

I first sent the finished compilation to very close friends, a super-supportive fan base. Then I expanded to a wider circle:

former teachers, an ex, several once dear but now distant friends. I dithered over sending a copy to a revered senior colleague, as we'd had a bumpy three-decade relationship. Finally, however, I mailed it, then panicked on the way home from the post office.

A week later I received an email from her with high praise and "thanks for the guffaws." She also recounted a heartfelt tale of fraught interactions with a teenager who unexpectedly joined her household, which she reflected on after reading my version. Her sincere, revealing email was heartening. I was glad I had taken the risk.

I've been okay during the pandemic because I'm a hermit at heart and because my retirement preceded Zoom's takeover of academia. Even as I have turned inward, though, my book has allowed me to reveal myself in a candid and meaningful way. My essays range from ruminating on why the world of Thomas the Tank Engine is 95% male or wondering whether I could get rich quick by following the well-established formula for writing summer-on-Nantucket chicklit, to pieces about coping with chronic illness. One essay reveals a close call with suicidal ideation. In conversation, I'm not sure I would have ever gone there, even with old friends. Writing made it easier. My readers' wide-ranging reactions have been Not as Expected, different than expected, often deeper than expected. We're closer now. And I've learned to expect more, of myself.

## TONY HOZENY

**Tony Hozeny** is the author of the novels *Driving Wheel* and *My House Is Dark* as well as numerous short stories, three of which were published in the past year. Tony has an MA from the Johns Hopkins Writing Seminars and taught creative writing at several colleges. He plays mandolin for the Northern Comfort Bluegrass Band. He is married with three children and three grandchildren.

# SHOCK AND ART

Tony Hozeny

In April 2020, I learned that I had both an aggressive, highly recurrent bladder cancer and a steadily-growing prostate cancer. To me, the word cancer has always meant "get ready to die." I'd have another surgery late in May to determine whether the cancer had invaded the bladder wall. If it had, the only treatment was to remove both bladder and prostate. If not, both cancers might respond to treatment. I had six weeks to absorb concepts like stoma and catheter and infusion therapy and radiation, six weeks to hope and worry.

My surgeon had a plan to address my two cancers. The plan might fail, but at least there was a plan.

There was no plan for COVID, a sinister force exploding across a poorly led, utterly unprepared nation and then exploding in hundreds of thousands of lungs, carried everywhere invisibly, even by healthy neighbors. So we hid, my wife and I, most painfully from children and grandchildren. COVID, far more than cancer, made me feel imminent, suffocating death.

I wished I could write, escape into a safe, imaginary world. But no words would come.

Sick of being cooped up, I drove into the Wisconsin countryside: cool blue sky and green sheen of buds on the maple and ash tree branches, winter finally receding like the small snow piles deep in the pines. Horses and dairy cattle grazed on hay bales. Farmers plowed the sour ground. A roadside mechanic wearing a tool belt lifted the hood of an old gray Cadillac. I thought about my three writing tools: language, memories, imagination. The wonderfully elastic and expressive English language stood faithfully by, as always. But I'd let life struggles dim my memories and blank out my imagination.

I slowed to enter a small town where a dozen new grain cars stood on the rail line. The sun flashing on these bright gray cars made me remember boyhood summers in the rail yards— hot wind, smoke and oil and cinders, switch engines chugging and steel couplers banging as we jumped boxcars for a slow ride down the line. I especially remembered one muggy afternoon hiding out with a girl on a railroad bridge: first cigarette, our choking and goofy laughter, first time sharing real secrets, first taste of a girl's soft, teasing lips. I couldn't wait to get to my keyboard.

The usual advice in crisis is to live one day at a time, keep your head down, plod along, forget dreams and possibilities---advice that has always chilled me. But as I began typing, I felt my words reclaiming what disease had taken or might take. I felt my life open out again. My healing came not from escaping into an imaginary world but from using my gift with words, respecting the craft of writing, and doing the work. A writer's job is to write, regardless of personal circumstance. I wrote about boyhood and COVID and faded love and grandchildren and cancer and death, six stories in four months, two of which were published. Perhaps those stories can help someone else heal.

# MARSHALL KARP

After a career as an award-winning writer, creative director and agency president in advertising, **Marshall Karp** turned to writing for the stage, screen, television, and finally, novels. In addition to his theatre and film credits he is the author of the critically acclaimed Lomax and Biggs Mysteries and the co-creator and co-author (along with James Patterson) of the #1 bestselling NYPD Red series.

# VITAMIN ANGELS

Marshall Karp

At 8:46 a.m. on Tuesday September 11, 2001 my daughter Sarah had just arrived at the World Trade Center when American Airlines flight 11 crashed into the North Tower.

An eternity would pass before I knew she survived, and the agony of watching the towers collapse until I got the joyful news was unbearable.

Thirty-six hours later I finally got to see Sarah, and that first embrace has forever been enshrined in our father-daughter chronicles as The Best Hug Ever.

As I held her in my arms, I made a vow. Do something. Pay the universe back for sparing my child.

I didn't have a plan. But a year later the opportunity presented itself. I live in Woodstock, New York, which has so many acupuncturists, homoeopathists, herbalists, and mind-body-spirit practitioners that we are the unofficial Woo-Woo Doctor Capital of the Western World.

My chiropractor invited me to meet with a group of his alternative medical cohorts to talk about an idea they were kicking around: collect vitamins and distribute them in countries where children are in dire need of nutritional supplements.

I had just retired from the advertising business, and I told them I knew people in the health care industry.

"We'll take their pills," someone said," "but we're not going to help them shill their drugs."

"No problem, but they'll want to have a say in where their contributions go." Instant uproar. "Nobody tells us how to do things."

I tried to explain corporate culture. All they heard was corporate oppression. I walked away.

But I couldn't walk away from their mission. I had found my purpose. I wanted to distribute vitamins to children in need. All I had to do was figure out how.

So I dialed up the Internet. Remember dial-up? Searching the web in those days was slow going, but I finally stumbled on this guy Howard Schiffer in Santa Barbara, California. I called. Howard had worked in the natural foods business. In 1994, he'd gotten an emergency call and delivered supplements to thousands of victims of the Northridge earthquake. And on that day Vitamin Angels was born.

For the next eight years Howard found companies willing to donate vitamins that were perfectly good, but too close to their 'Sell By' date to ship to retailers. By the time I called him he was distributing them through a local relief group to 20 countries. And he was doing it alone. Without a salary.

I asked him what was the biggest global problem that vitamins could solve? "Five hundred thousand children around the world go blind from Vitamin A deficiency," he said. "We know the solution — a high dose of Vitamin A administered every six months. It would only cost twenty-five cents a year to save one child's life. But we don't have the money."

"I know people with money," I said. "And I can write."

So I wrote. Proposals, impassioned cover letters, and eventually I wrote six words that would galvanize people to action. Be an Angel. Save a Life.

It worked. Johnson and Johnson gave us $250,000, and our program to eradicate Vitamin A deficiency childhood blindness on the planet was underway. The mission continues. The scope has evolved. Last year alone, Vitamin Angels distributed life-saving vitamins to 60 million kids, women and babies in seventy countries.

And I still write for them.

Two decades have passed since my daughter was at Ground Zero. The memory is still painful but knowing that the thousands of words I've written for Vitamin Angels has saved the children of other parents diminishes the pain.

Howard Schiffer is a global humanitarian. I'm just a writer. But every time we talk he reminds me of the impact that my voice has made.

Like a lot of writers, I don't handle praise well. So I just tell him to shut up and save it for the eulogy.

## ANN LEVIN

**Ann Levin** is a writer and editor who worked for many years as a journalist, including as national news editor at The Associated Press. Before that, she was a reporter for several newspapers in Texas and California. She continues to review books for the Associated Press as well as for *USA Today*, and has been working on a memoir, two chapters of which were published in the online magazines Sensitive Skin and Southeast Review. She has also performed on stage with the New York-based writers' group Read650. Visit annlevinwriter.com to see her work.

# TWO GREEN NOTEBOOKS

Ann Levin

I was diagnosed with stage three stomach cancer on a bright spring morning in 2004. In the crazy days that followed, I updated my will, put my accounts in Stan's name, took a medical leave of absence from work, and consulted with teams of doctors at two different hospitals.

But before any of that happened, I went to the fanciest stationery store on the Upper East Side and bought two green Clairefontaine notebooks—one to take notes in whenever I spoke to the doctors, and one to write down my daily medications, treatments and test results, and what Stan and I referred to as my "odd sensations."

That fall, I remember my hair falling out and how I took to covering my bald head with silk scarves and thinking that I was still among the least-weird-looking people on the streets of New York. I remember how the chemo made certain odors unbearable, even ones that are normally pleasant, like the pine

49

boughs that decorate our building at Christmas and the vats of soup at the Hale & Hearty restaurant near the clinic where I was treated.

And all through those four months of treatment and five years of follow-up, which included a never-ending battery of endoscopies, colonoscopies, PET scans, and bloodwork, I took meticulous notes, kept all my bills and lab reports, and filed away every article that had any bearing whatsoever on the diagnosis, treatment and prognosis of different kinds of cancer.

I wish I could tell you that instead, I'd written a poignant, funny graphic memoir like the cartoonist Marisa Acocella Marchetto. Or a Marxist feminist critique of the medical industrial complex like the poet and essayist Anne Boyer. Or a profound meditation on the meaning of life like the neurosurgeon Paul Kalanithi, who died before his manuscript for *When Breath Becomes Air* was finished.

But I didn't. What I did write amounts to more than a shopping list, but less than a diary, and certainly nothing as formal or elegant or considered as a memoir. The messy pages, many of them dog-eared, chronicle these facts: that a week before the operation, Stan and I drove to the Target at the Queens Place Mall so I could buy a nightgown, bathrobe, and slippers to wear in the hospital. That my wallet was stolen from a locker in my hospital room the day after my surgery. And that once, after radiation, I was so exhausted and depleted that I took a two-hour nap after walking up the hill on 94th Street between Second and Third Avenue.

None of what I wrote would mean anything to anyone but me. It's like the scratches that people leave on the walls of their prison cells, simply a device to mark the passage of time. I suppose you could say that I was a prisoner too—of my body, which was occupied by out-of-control cancer cells, and of the doctors, who teed up the most powerful machines and poisons on earth to do battle against the rogue invaders.

It took me a long, long time before I was blasé enough about the experience to put the green notebooks away in a drawer. Even now, they're precious to me, the scribbles on paper adding up to five years of my life.

They remind me of a time when my friends and family came here to take me to doctors' appointments and hang out with me in the chemo suite. When people I barely knew sent me cards and flowers and recommended all kinds of books by cancer survivors. When, in a nation with unequal access to health care, I had good insurance, a kind boss, and some of the best doctors on the planet.

Measuring just a little over 5-by-8 inches, the two wire-bound green notebooks tell a very simple story: that something truly awful happened to me once, and I survived it.

# STEVEN LEWIS

**Steven Lewis** is a former mentor at SUNY-Empire State College, long-time member of the Sarah Lawrence College Writing Institute faculty, and longtime freelancer. His work has been published widely, from the notable to the beyond obscure, including a biblically long list of parenting publications (seven kids, sixteen grandkids). He is a Contributing Writer at *Talking Writing Magazine* and Senior Editor/Literary Ombudsman for the spoken word venue Read650. A new novel, *The Lights Around the Shore*, will be published in 2021 by Moonshine Cove.

# INTO THE CREEK

Steven Lewis

From a mechanical hospital bed in the Beaufort Memorial ICU, gurgling and pulsing noises all around, I begin my journey with IV drips in my arm, oxygen cannula up my nose, intermittent pneumatic compression cuffs on my legs, a kind but unrecognizable nurse in a mask, gown, and gloves turning me one way then the other so she can change the sheets, then handing me unidentified pills, which I swallow obediently like some hapless child or dispirited rheumy-eyed old man, agreeing without protest to anything I am offered: jello, Mucinex, Tylenol, thermometer, dry chicken, the daily shot in my stomach ...

... remembrances of my late friend Neil passing in the air, how he was being buried alive in his fading body from ALS; how he wrote every day during that last year of life with breathtaking bravery and grace; how at some desolate point with the last finger he could move, and closer to the end through computer-trained retinas. How he shared his remarkable vision from inside that cocoon, the ten-inch gap he'd see every morning through the bedroom window, peering down past his feet, unable to move a toe until the nurse would come to wash and turn and dress him.

Unlike Neil, though, I cannot see past the haze or lift a finger to write anything at all. Not even a text to my worried children. Days seem to pass or not pass as through a dream or hallucination and I follow whatever appears over my bed, float along with it until it escapes my sight, and unable to pin the words on a page like beautiful butterflies, I watch them flutter off beyond memory.

Weeks later, as I lay alone in my marital bed in near helpless isolation, I recall—or imagine—or make up—how I had been peering vacantly out the hospital window one evening when Neil appeared, sat down beside me, not to offer the usual clichéd consolations or encouragements, which I know now would have caused him to disappear into useless ether, but only to share the narrow view through the window with me, the private and solitary darkness now illuminated for both of us.

Perhaps it was a dream. Perhaps a dream of a dream. It's even possible I conjured it through foggy recollections in poetry I wrote months later, but I'm telling you here that as Neil and I watched headlights passing down Ribaud Road in front of the hospital, I took one shallow inspiration after another, after another, chest rising, chest falling, each breath drawn from Neil's long silenced voice I could then hear in a pitch that would travel with me beyond the ICU to a light blue cottage on Duck Blind Alley in Port Royal, fourteen feet wide, white trim herons, gators, and turtles in the pond across the way, Spanish moss swaying from massive live oaks outside my window, a tiny library out front on London Avenue, Sands Beach beyond the marshes.

And in that weariness beyond weariness, thirty pounds lighter but better able to slip through the shredded chrysalis of that virus to hear a far-off call, not a barbaric yawp, not a voice crying in the wilderness, only the echo of Neil's sweet smirky laugh as I drop my oars into a creek that has appeared beside my bed, first drifting away from the sickly despair that rises out of a transactional life, then rowing with the current toward some kind of health not defined by illness, sounds beginning to flow through my heaving arms, the creak and clunk of oarlocks, words appearing between ripples on the surface of the water, forming sentences that do not pretend to make life easier or harder, better or worse, sensible or insensible, only to turn a misty beam of light ten inches ahead to where the current is taking me.

# DAVID MASELLO

**David Masello** began his career as a nonfiction book editor at Simon and Schuster, then went on to hold senior editorial positions at many magazines, including *Travel & Leisure, Art & Antiques,* and *Town & Country.* He's currently executive editor of *Milieu,* a magazine about design and architecture. He's a widely published essayist and poet, with pieces appearing in the *New York Times, Best American Essays,* and numerous literary and art magazines. He is the author of two books about art and architecture.

# A MOONLIGHT RIDE

David Masello

I'd been told the horse I was to mount for the trail ride would stop at every flowering jacaranda tree to sample blossoms.

"When Moonlight does that, raise your heel, hit him hard in the flank," the guide said astride her saddle, hoisting her boot at a sharp angle and jamming it just short of her horse's side. "Only way to get him to stop. To get moving, do it again. Same action, for stopping and starting."

I knew I'd not be able to do that.

When Moonlight was led from his stall, I petted the hard plane of his mane, hot and bony. He seemed indifferent to my touch. I felt insulted. I was showing him affection, but unlike a dog, no reciprocity or acknowledgment. Then I thought, how bored Moonlight must be following the same trail every day, carrying a tourist like myself who knew nothing about how to ride.

Hitched in the saddle, I noticed a deeply incised brand on his rump, a chili-pepper, cartoonish—with lines radiating outward to indicate spiciness.

I asked the guide about the inkless-tattoo.

"Moonlight had a past before he came here. Different name, too. After the ride, I'll tell you."

Moonlight picked his way along the narrow, boulder-strewn trail. I rocked astride him, and despite what the guide said, I had no control over him. I knew nothing about horses but could tell he'd do as he wanted.

The first time I'd been to Arizona, I was with my then-partner—the one-who-got-away-in-my-life, as the saying goes. On a desert backroad, we came to a sign announcing the site before us, the Great Painted Desert. The copy stated the hewn valley before us was the size of Connecticut. We stood beside our car, looking into the hazy distance, visoring a hand over our eyes, unable to discern the site's stated scale. Then, as if simultaneously looking through binoculars and adjusting the knob to focus, we saw what we were told we'd see: A space the size of a state, perimeters discernible.

I still invoke that site. Look closely enough at any situation of distress, you'll see its full scope. Understand its dimensions, you can solve it.

Moonlight has.

Moonlight clomped along, head down, as if he'd followed this route a thousand times—which he might have—negotiating inclines, edged with thorns of prickly-pear.

The moment we entered pure desert, Moonlight stopped. So fast I slid nearly off my mount. Moonlight swung his head and began to eat blossoms from a tree.

The guide had been talking about ancient metate we'd be passing—granite slabs, mica aglint, where Indian women had ground mesquite pods with such diligence over centuries that bowl-like depressions formed within stones.

She trotted over. "Hard in the flank," she reiterated. "He's had worse in his life."

I dug my boot heel too gently into his dulled brown flesh. Moonlight continued eating voraciously, undisturbed, blossom after blossom dissolving into his mouth.

The guide lifted her leg and jabbed a spurred-boot heel into his body. He whinnied, threw his head back, a blossom stuck to his wet, flaring nostrils.

"Moonlight's difficult," the guide explained. "When we adopted him, he was so wild his owner branded him with a chili-pepper to mark him as untamable. He's even branded underneath, same symbol, as if that would've taught him. The flesh there, a lot thinner. That must have hurt. Bad. Moonlight was on his way to being glue."

"Why, Moonlight," I asked.

"When he came here, he'd stay awake in the stable and even if we had him in the corral outside. He'd look at the moon, whinnying at it. Like he was talking to it."

Moonlight continued along the trail, edged by arroyos, smooth as pottery, unimpressed with the story he'd heard many times about himself. Up ahead, a jacaranda appeared, a stilled purple firework ablaze in the monochromatic desert, and Moonlight raised his head, his tongue already out.

# MARGARITA MEYENDORFF

**Margarita Meyendorff** is the author of the published memoir *DP: Displaced Person*. The daughter of a Russian Baron, she was born displaced in a refugee camp in Germany, far from the opulence of Imperial Russia. A series of wars destroyed this privileged existence and Margarita's life became a series of extraordinary moves. She has performed as an actress, dancer, musician, and storyteller at venues throughout the United States and in Europe, and her memoir is being translated for publication in Russia. Margarita has recently published *Flipping the Bird,* an anthology of short stories based on her numerous life adventures.

# ABSENT

Margarita Meyendorff

Why did I start my day crying? Outside, sleet needled the windowpane as I settled into my large armchair by the fireplace to write, hoping that by doing so, I would summon up a remedy and overcome a nagging feeling of hopelessness and depression. What was so wrong, for so long?

Sadness made tears, unbidden, brim in my eyes. I recalled the years when after my divorce, my two children and I struggled to survive on our own. The responsibility of caring for them overwhelmed me, and I coped but I also ran. I ran to menial jobs. I ran to graduate school. I ran to buy fast food at the market. I ran to dance classes. I ran to lovers. I ran from darkness and anxiety. Most desperately and destructively, I ran away from myself and I ran away from my children.

The running took its toll. I thought I had lost my son, Jarett, when at age eight, he went to live with his father. Two years later, he returned from France, depressed when his father's second marriage fell apart. Jessie, my daughter, suffered abandonment issues when her father showed his blatant preference for his son over his daughter. Jessie had remained with me, but our relationship was shaky, at best. She was depressed and I couldn't help her. I was too busy surviving.

I wrote down the truth, the cause of my lack of hope as a chapter in my then memoir-in-progress, DP: Displaced Person. Even while loving them, I had abandoned my children. The truth frightened me; fear brought anxiety which almost paralyzed me. Somehow, I found the strength to continue. I had to get it all down and as I continued, I felt the stirrings of an optimism. Was I finding a way to heal the damage?

By mid-morning I finished writing the chapter and re-read it. I became overwhelmed with grief and at the same time, a tremendous feeling of love for my children enveloped me. The craziness of these mixed emotions propelled me to stand up from my comfortable chair, put on my coat and hat and climb into my car.

Sobbing, I drove the eight miles to where Jessie lived. She climbed into my car and we drove to a secluded place near her home where we could talk. I turned my tear-stained face to Jessie and asked for her forgiveness. It didn't matter that years had gone by and Jessie was fine and standing on her feet. I hoped for her forgiveness. I needed her to know that I felt to blame for her struggles in adolescence' that I had abandoned her when she needed me most.

We spoke about that time—what it was like for both of us. She forgave me; we cried, we hugged, we became closer.

Then I drove to the shop where my son Jarett worked. In a corner of a small room where the tie-dye clothing he designed hung to dry, I asked him to forgive me for not being more present in his life. Should I have forbade him to go live with his father? After witnessing two divorces, Jarett had become disillusioned with love. He felt he lost his family and grew more silent. For a while he had turned to drugs. Now, Jarett and I spoke of love and I admitted my deepest regrets. He forgave and we, too, became closer.

That freezing morning, I had no idea that writing the chapter "Absent" would hurl me into an anguish of truth-telling and inspire a faint hope that was fulfilled in forgiveness. This time, I did not run away but believed that by persevering and facing the demons, I might heal these fraught relationships with my children and reverse the pain.

That morning, I wrote myself a better chapter in my life.

## LEAH MOORE

**Leah Moore** is a high school English and theater teacher, with fifteen years of experience in New York. She is a mom of three and an advocate for individuals with special needs. She is working to shift the narrative to create more stories, centering around individuals with disabilities, through her writing and her blog www.lovingyoubig. com. Her first memoir, *Loving You Big*, will be released in August 2021.

# HOW DO YOU DO IT ALL?

Leah Moore

"I really don't know how you do it all."

This is the most common statement I hear as a mother. I am hoping it is said so often because three loud children are a noticeable handful, and not because one of those children has significant special needs. Because then the comment becomes less of a compliment and more of a placeholder for "I couldn't do what you do and I'm fortunate I don't have to." And it reduces my child with a disability to just her disability, and that is not okay. Since I don't have enough information to know if I am being praised or pitied, I just politely smile and leave.

When you become a special needs parent, you'll often hear that old cliché: put your oxygen mask on first. The message is important; before you can take care of anyone else, you need to first take care of yourself. The problem is, I found a loophole. I found a way to survive with catch breaths, shallow sips of air like I'd use in singing.

Holding my breath became my mom's badge of honor. I convinced myself I was an excellent multitasker and if I worked fast enough, I would never have to admit I was on my way to suffocating.

The only space where I didn't flounder was the classroom where I teach. It was where I was truly separated from home and where I remembered the person I was before. When the students in my ninth-grade English class were working on a personal narrative unit, I wanted to model the assignment. So one evening, after my kids had finally gone to bed, I wearily sat down at the computer, frustrated that I had added more to my plate, and tried to write. I started typing and an entire memoir poured out of me.

The stories kept coming. With each story, I found a way to put into words what I had only been swallowing in silence. It was how I reconciled the tension between being a teacher of words and having a child who might never use them. It was how I assuaged my guilt about not attending another birthday party because the rigorous therapy schedule didn't give us time. It was how I organized myself after the birth of my twins, and then privately handled each of their medical scares. The more the words showed up on paper, the less I carried the weight of them.

I've always had the sensation to write; I just never knew what subject to choose. The circumstances of my life shifted this view of writing. The more I captured the stories of my family, the more I was able to notice the moments of joy, even

haos. I replaced eating chocolate in the bathroom with
ng in the basement. I learned it was not just possible for
to take a moment for myself, it was necessary. My husband
ntly put my daughter to bed as I released a sentence from
rain. I jotted down notes as twin B rested on my head to
h PAW Patrol. I held twin A while I dictated ideas.

Through writing, I learned to live in a way that allowed
o pay attention to where my stories were hiding. I learned I
he most like myself when I wrote. On paper, I can respond
e comments I hear in public. On paper, I can make sure
ak the truth. On paper, I have time. Writing has finally
n me an answer to that dreaded question about how I do

## JOHN MITCHELL MORRIS

**John Mitchell Morris** was born in Corpus Christi, Texas, and is a graduate of California State University, Northridge (BA), Villanova University Charles Widger School of Law (JD), and Sarah Lawrence College (MFA). A lawyer and former actor, he is the chair of college writing at Purchase College. His debut novel, *In the Trembling Heart*, is a love story set in the early twenty-first century that explores the intersections of tragedy, art, and redemption. He lives in Bronxville, New York and Los Angeles.

# THE POWER TO CREATE

John Mitchell Morris

"Are you watching?" I said, five lines into the scene. The question, however, was not scripted, and my indignance had nothing to do with the dim teenager for whom I was auditioning, who I, at twenty-eight, was ridiculously too old to play.

The casting director looked up from her phone. "What are you—?"

"You told my agent it was urgent I read for this part. I cancelled my flight to my friend's wedding this morning so I could read for you this afternoon. The least you can do is pay attention."

In Hollywood, those with power, however limited, grow so accustomed to being brown-nosed and flattered, their reactions to any treatment short of groveling arrive in slow motion and with visible shock.

"I'm—sorry," she said. "Do you want to start again, Nick?"

"My name is Mitch."

"Right. Sorry. Let's start again."

And we did, though needless to say, I didn't get the part. But this scene marked the end of my eight-year willingness to subject myself to the daily frustration and humiliation of the actor's pursuit. Though I'd worked consistently, to often I'd found myself the runner up of castings, the veritable bridesmaid at the altar of parts that kept launching my competitors into career-changing roles. Over the years, the agents, managers, acting coaches, publicists, and imaging consultants that had guided me had expressed different ideas about who I was or who I should be. One manager suggested I spend more time tanning and developing my pecs. One acting coach told me I should shadow my cowboy cousin in Texas and adopt his mannerisms as my own; she laughed when I asked if I could calf-rope her. One agent held nothing back in her assessment of why I couldn't break through: "Maybe if you weren't so faggy," she said on the phone, as I approached the red light at Highland and Melrose, stunned and numb. But I didn't hang up thinking poorly of her. I felt ashamed for having failed to create a product that others could sell, and to hide a part of me I'd struggled with long before I'd fled Texas.

But above all, I'd allowed the business to destroy my love for acting and the love of creating I'd exhibited since childhood.

After I moved to Philadelphia to attend law school, the demons of those LA years treaded the darkest corners of my doubts, as I sat up late trying to understand why the issue of A's children's issue cannot inherit Black Acre in fee due to the Rule of Perpetuities. I also wondered if I cared. But in the solitude and immersive reading and writing necessary for the study of law, the drumbeat of my artistic nature led me back to the mammoth novels I'd absorbed as a teenager and then toward the excellence of Henry James, Proust, and Balzac. Soon I was writing my own novel, putting to good use those years of scene study. Even while practicing law, after head-spinning days in court and drafting motions until my eyes wetted and blurred, I arrived home at night and continued developing the characters that lived in my heart, as the glow of my desk lamp lit the portals of my imagination.

After seven years of writing and rewriting, I completed my first novel early this year. What the future holds for it is uncertain; the transition from creation to commodification is daunting and has long mystified even those writers our fingertips reach for each time we near our bookshelves. But unlike the career-changing role I needed as a young actor, my writing life is not driven by a result. The desire to create is a pure desire, born out of love and in defiance of the world's cruelty and indifference. As a writer, I need audition for no one. I can play all the parts. The power to create is mine.

# ANTHONHY MURPHY

**Anthony C. Murphy** has worked and performed on the open mic/ spoken word scene in the UK and New York City for the last twelve years. He has written several poetry chapbooks, two illustrated childrens' books and a novel, *Shiftless*, published by Atmosphere Press. He was most recently published in *The Westchester Review* and *The Long Islander*. He lives by the Hudson River in Yonkers with his family and two dogs.

# STEADY

Anthony Murphy

Our new house was a red brick semi, it had a small home-made driveway, and many other do-it-yourself features that needed fixing. It did have a back garden, although one with a massive mound of mud that my wife Lou said I could remove to create a patio. Projects! We had our first mortgage and our first house. I was 23 years old. I started digging.

Digging, I found a tortoise skeleton in the mound. I was confused. Where do you bury inconsequential bones that you'd just dug up?

We were only there a week before Lou went into labor. She had loved being pregnant. Happy to eat and loll at the end. She'd been through it once before and our little Frank was two and a half now and ready for someone to lovingly beat with his worldly knowledge.

That night Lou went to the hospital with me driving. Her mum looked after Frank. I thought I could deal with it as we had midwives that we knew.

Lou tore herself inside out giving birth. Johnny came out fine and was swabbed, swaddled, and placed in my arms for a minute but Lou's placenta was still attached to the uterus and all of that came out in front of us. She was trying to look down and wonder what was going on as the midwives dithered. They tried to push parts back inside as Lou looked at me holding our healthy newborn kid and I noticed all the blood and we all knew that something was not right. But it was happening.

Lou was angry; I could see that she was. I couldn't even tell her to breathe. She looked me right in the eye, held my gaze, and didn't say a word. Shook her head at the ridiculousness of the situation. She wasn't angry with me. We were together, but she was the one in peril. She knew I couldn't help. We both saw how much blood was on the table and heard that they couldn't reach a surgeon. I still had the baby in my arms and tried to keep eye contact with Lou. We just looked at each other and waited as she kept shaking her head slowly.

Eventually an anesthetist turned up and he calmed the whole situation. Lou was grateful for him but there were still problems. She had lost a lot of blood and the uterus was not inside her body. They took her away - to operate. They took the baby away, too.

I went home. I phoned Lou's mother and I phoned my mother and I cried and I said I needed their help.

We were all at the hospital the next day but Lou was in the ICU so we couldn't see her. She wasn't good. They said she had lost eight pints of blood and they had to give her a hysterectomy. She was stabilizing and had to stay in for a week at least.

I remembered the look on Lou's face then: there was anger but also resignation. I can't speak for her, but knowing her, there was already the thought of retribution. She was giving me a signal to get the bastards that had done this. Whether they be the non-existent gods or the incompetent scientists. She was mad that it could even happen. And what do you do against such forces? Because all she wanted was another baby.

I got to take Johnny the next day. I fed him and his brother, with two grandmas' help, until Lou came home.

Lou recovered on our couch for a few months more while I finished the patio. I'm not a quick worker. Time slowed for all of us. We had a tortoise. skeleton watching from the bookshelf. We had made a home and grown a family out of this mess.

## MARTHA NANCE

**Martha Nance** is a physician in Minnesota who specializes in Parkinson's disease and Huntington's disease, two conditions for which we do not yet have a satisfactory answer. Although most of her previous work has appeared in scientific journals such as *Journal of Parkinson's Disease* and *The American Journal of Medical Genetics*, she has recently balanced those medical pieces with essays in *Intima: A Journal of Narrative Medicine* and *Dreamer's Creative Writing,* among others. Her photographs have also been published in a variety of literary journals.

# DIARY

Martha Nance

**March 2020**. I get a call from a patient's wife. "Dr. Nance, you know Jim's Parkinson's disease had gotten so bad. Last week he developed a fever and trouble breathing, caught that Corona infection they keep talking about, but we weren't allowed to see him in the nursing home. Since his room was on the first floor, we gathered outside his window to sing hymns. We held up his brand-new granddaughter so he could see her, and we could see that he was smiling. He died two days later."

I bake a birthday torte for my thirty-two-year-old son—gluten-free for his wife, chocolate for him—and mail it to his New England apartment.

**April 2020**. I receive a frantic call from another wife. Fred, a patient and a former colleague, was confused and sleepy after a fall. I arrange the admission, and Fred's not-yet-retired partner, Dr. Davidson, meets him at the hospital door to help him through the admitting process (wives not allowed)! A large brain hemorrhage and a few conversations later, Fred passes peacefully, his grieving wife heartened by the compassionate act of his colleague.

I plant lobelias and alyssum in my greenhouse; in a few weeks, they will explode in blue and violet drops of honey-sweetness.

**May 2020**. My city explodes in flames and anger. The hospital where my husband works, only a few blocks from the epicenter of the George Floyd humanity quake, is boarded up and noncritical patients diverted elsewhere. My husband participates in emergency Zoom meetings about how to manage the dual crises of COVID and riots.

I take hundreds of photographs of a burbling outdoor fountain, an infinite set of moments of light, motion, and texture. Later I brighten, crop, filter, and recolor them, revealing the ideas and feelings hidden within. Tonight's photo-paintings are red and dark, disordered and angry.

**August 2020**. Several of my patients have survived COVID-19 infections; many others have not left their homes since February. But they appear in the obituaries nonetheless. Are they dying of loneliness and fear?

When you creep through the field, camera in hand, to within inches of a cool dragonfly, waiting for the rising sun to catch the dewdrops on her eye, laundry, groceries, and upcoming lectures all magically vanish.

**October 2020**. I visit my eighty-seven-year-old father in his Memory Care Unit. Puffing at his end of the long table separating us, he removes his mask, wondering why he has it on in the first place. He is pretty sure that I have children, and wants to know what they are doing, where they are living. We will review this again next week, as we did last week.

Homemade fudge is the solution. After several tries, I finally find the Best Recipe, and successfully elicit smiles!

**December 2020**. The end of a long year. The bell has tolled seventy-five times for my patients.

Greeting card stores do not provide condolence cards in bulk. I order a box of add-your-own-photo cards, on which I have placed a photograph of a setting sun. Perhaps my note is helpful to families, but should I admit that it mostly provides closure for me?

**February 2021**. My son calls. He and his wife have been diagnosed with COVID-19. They have food, Tylenol, and a cat. Suppressing my instincts to fly out to "mother" them, I simply call every day, fingers crossed.

A COVID Care Package, including Best Recipe fudge, makes its way to the East Coast.

**March 2021**. My father has gotten his vaccines, as have my husband and I. My son and his wife are on the mend. Twelve more patients have died. Lobelia and alyssum bloom happily in the greenhouse. Larval dragonflies await spring's warmth to sprout wings, while our hospitals hope their "diversity initiatives" will also take flight. After a springlike weekend, winter has returned, and I take my camera outside in search of snowflakes.

# IRENE O'GARDEN

**Irene O'Garden** has won or been nominated for prizes in nearly every writing category from stage to e-screen, hardcovers, as well as literary magazines and anthologies. Her critically-acclaimed play *Women On Fire*, (Samuel French) played sold-out houses at Off-Broadway's Cherry Lane Theatre. O'Garden won a Pushcart Prize for her lyric essay "Glad To Be Human," featured in her new book of essays by that name published by Mango (May 2020.) Mango also published her memoir *Risking the Rapids: How My Wilderness Journey Healed My Childhood*. O'Garden's poems and essays have been featured in dozens of literary journals and anthologies.

# THE OLD SHAPESHIFTER

Irene O'Garden

"You could be another Bette Davis," said my college acting teacher. That and my passionate, spiritual devotion to the theater catapulted me to glamorous New York City.

To waitress. To shovel my tips to a headshot photographer. To scour the smudgy pages of "Backstage" for auditions. To line up in dim and smelly halls on cattle calls, and yes, at last to nab some good roles here and there.

Then a sparkling review in *Variety*! I'm spiralling up. An agent's out there. Just keep at it. Work those graveyard shifts, tap dance on our parquet floors, run audition pieces. All worth it because this art form is a healing holy thing. Theatre had lifted me from crushing family pains, given me identity. Friends. Developed my body, my voice, my mind, my spirit. I would thank it with a lifetime of dedication.

Finally, I win the brilliant role that'll tip me into the golden circle of working actors: Madam Arkadina in *The Seagull*. (No matter that she's middle-aged and I'm in my twenties. I positively ooze gravitas.) Okay, maybe not a paying gig. But a great showcase.

The venue's no great shakes (a hole in an upstairs wall on stinky fourteenth Street.) But Chekhov!

First rehearsal's a bit odd. Our young director Marissa enters wearing actual jodhpurs and a white silk scarf à la Cecil B. DeMille. "On your feet," she says. "We're going to block the show."

That's like saying "Firemen, jump on the truck," without introducing them to each other or the equipment. We fumble with scripts as we stumble around. Another alas: she's cast her painfully unattractive boyfriend as my dashingly handsome love interest. Okay. I can act.

We soon discover he has no facility with language and no experience on stage. Okay, I'll act for two. This play is my shot.

Every spare moment I memorize lines. No use sweating the small stuff.

Second rehearsal: although we have yet to even read through the script together, Marissa reblocks the show, changing even the placement of entrances and exits. One of us gently asks her if she's ever directed before. "It's my second show," she proudly declares.

By now we seasoned actors are stealing looks at one another, sidling up and muttering, "Wanna go for coffee after?"

Sans the boyfriend, over bitter java, we agree the show will be a fiasco unless we take matters into our own hands. We schedule scenework with each other and promise vigilance. I can act for two. We can direct ourselves. It is Chekhov and it is my chance.

At the third rehearsal I'm offstage running my lines at the grungy front desk when my eye falls on piles of flyers. *Dirty Work at The Crossroads. A Melodrama.* 7:30 pm at this theater on exactly the same days our Seagull is to play.

At break, I take the flyer in my anger-trembling hand. "Marissa, what's the deal? This is our time slot!"

"Oh, our show goes on at 10 pm."

"No one's gonna watch Chekov at 10 pm after a melodrama!" I'd act for two, direct myself, supply my own costumes, but not for no audience.

As it turned out, neither would anyone else. The cast quit as one, even as Marissa wailed, "You're killing my seagull!" I spent dark weeping weeks trying to revive the thudded mass of feathers that had been my winged dream, my heart, my art, but I knew at last I had to give it up. I'd recently read a resonant sentence: If it's not fun, stop doing it.

I was miserable. I went to an artist colony to lick my wounds with watercolor. Emotions rose. I wrote them down. I didn't have to wait to be cast to write or to paint. Suddenly I saw that art had not abandoned me. The old shapeshifter just changed form. The only thing to heal a broken art? Another art.

# JENNIFER RAWLINGS

**Jennifer Rawlings** is an award-winning writer, performer, and film-maker who has appeared on Comedy Central, CMT, PBS, VH-1, A&E, CNN, HLN, and in the film, *I Am Battle Comic*. She has two popular TEDx talks, and her solo show, *I Only Smoke in War Zones*, tours globally. Jennifer was named one of the "21 Change makers of the 21st Century" by Women's E News, and her directorial debut, *Forgotten Voices: Women in Bosnia*, screens at film festivals and universities worldwide. Rawlings has written for television, books, film, and for several publications including the *New York Times*. She is the proud mother of five.

# HOPE HAPPENS

Jennifer Rawlings

I've had plenty of problems.

I've lost people I love, almost died myself...twice, spent months in the hospital, married, divorced, married again. I have ridden on the financial rollercoaster without a seatbelt. I've known career chaos. And then there are my kids, four biological children and two children by marriage: my step-son and husband.

I have been traveling to war zones for twenty years to entertain the troops. Those travels prompted me to direct the documentary Forgotten Voices: Women in Bosnia. The film is about women and the aftermath of war. I interviewed dozens of women for the film. Different ages, religions, walks of life. Nejla is one who still walks with me.

Nejla lives in Mostar, Bosnia. Tarik, her oldest son, twenty-six, agreed to translate.

Tarik started the interview by introducing himself and his mother to the camera, kissing her on the cheek, saying "This is my mom and I love my mom."

Nejla told me about always being hungry during the war. Never knowing what was going to happen next. Always afraid about what was going to drop out of the sky.

Nejla began talking about her youngest son Emitas, born July 8, 1995, just a few months before the Bosnian war ended, and the Dayton Peace Accord was signed.

She talked about how Emitas loved Eminem and video games. I thought of my own boys; my son Noah is only six months older than Emitas. They like the same things.

Sitting behind the camera looking at Nejla I realized that we are just two moms talking about our boys. So when Nejla told me how Emitas loved doing homework, I thought about how I have to bribe, negotiate and threaten my boys to do homework.

When I asked Tarik to ask his mother to tell me what happened to Emitas, Tarik's eyes watered.

My hands began to shake, I could feel tiny beads of sweat pooling on the back of my neck as I asked Tarik again. "Please ask your mother to tell me what happened."

Tarik turned to his mother. He swallowed his trembling words, whispering the translated question to her.

Nejla covered her face with both hands, gasping for breath. She reached for a photograph of Emitas. Hugging the photograph to her bosom, she wept.

Then she said, "On October 28, 2004 (nine years after the war ended), Emitas came home from school, did his homework, then went outside to play soccer with his best friend.

"They were playing in an area where they had always played. An area on the map that was free and clear of landmines and munitions."

A few moments later, Nejla continued. "But the map was wrong. Someone left a grenade in the rocks. My son's friend picked it up.

"His friend died instantly. My son, my baby was two or three meters away. He was still alive when my husband got to him. But he lost too much blood and died on the way to the hospital."

Nejla tore a tissue in half, giving half to me as she continued.

When I could find words again, I asked, "Do you have any anger toward the people who left the grenade behind?"

Nejla caressed the photograph of Emitas.

"My son died in play. I have no space in my heart for anger, only love and loss of a child. If there is anyone in this world who can stop these things from happening, please help."

I used to get lost in my sadness. Since my conversation with Nejla, I don't do that anymore. It's not that I don't still feel the pain. I do.

But I've changed the way I deal with grief and disappointment, because the people I have met changed me, and the way I see the world. Hope happens when you refuse to let the world change you, and instead you change the world with love.

# LAUREL ROSS

**Laurel Ross** lives in Chicago where she is a writer, birder, prairie restoration volunteer, chorister (alto), Zen practitioner, and novice orchid enthusiast. A retired conservation ecologist, she is active in the Chicago live storytelling community. Currently working on a memoir that explores her youthful excesses, Laurel has recently discovered that composing daily haiku is an elegant way to merge her passions for nature, Zen, and poetry.

# GOOD SAMARITANS

Laurel Ross

Cruising my congested new neighborhood looking for a parking space, I was annoyed when the pickup truck ahead suddenly slowed down. Was he going to snag a spot before I got to it? No. He made a sharp left into the alley and as I accelerated I saw why. A large dark heap was positioned in the middle of Sunnyside, a narrow one-way street. Cars were parked on both sides and there was no way to avoid hitting it/him/her except to duck down the alley like the truck.   I   briefly considered backing up, but instead I looked closer to see what it was. A bulky woman dressed in black was sitting upright in the street surrounded by shopping bags--a surreal scene on a sunny spring day. She appeared to be alive. I turned off my engine, put on the blinkers, and walked over to her.

She looked right into my eyes.

"Do you need help?" I asked, knowing it was a stupid question.

She flailed her arms, struggling like an upside down beetle.

"My knees are broken," she wailed. A tattered facemask dangled from her chin. I realized that I had left my own mask in the car. I could almost see the droplets flying out of her mouth when she sputtered her words. My mind raced through all the newly issued directives from the governor, the mayor and the CDC: "Avoid contact with others. Maintain a distance of at least six feet." This was the beginning of the pandemic and I was still learning the rules of engagement.

Completely flummoxed and trying to buy time I lamely offered, "Let me move your things out of the street."

I was queasy touching her grocery bags and her huge leather purse, but it was easier than touching her.

"Can you roll onto your hands and knees and crawl?" I pleaded.

She wheezed.

I looked around. Why were no other cars arriving on the scene? How long had we been there?

The woman was not small and not strong and not positioned to be maneuvered easily, but there was no other choice. I gritted my teeth, gave her my hands and tried to heave her from her bum onto her feet.

After only a few seconds it was clear that I would never raise her. She was agitated and I was losing it.

As I phoned 911, cursing myself for not doing that immediately, I saw a short, dark young man emerging from the alley, briskly walking directly toward us as if to join the fray.

The pickup driver! He had stashed the truck and returned to help!

With his strength and my clumsy assistance, we pulled her upright. Her knees were not broken. She could stand. She could slowly walk.

"Where are you going?" She pointed to an apartment building fifty feet away, a building I can see from my dining room window. I moved her bags to the door. Her groceries were heavy—cans and bottles and a large box of cheap wine.

To her rescuer she said, "You are my angel. My angel."

"Should I call an ambulance?" the angel asked.

"No! No! No!"

At that moment my personal concern about intimate contact with an unhealthy-looking, unclean-smelling stranger overcame my impulse to help. The angel would get her home.

I raced to my car, sprayed disinfectant, parked and ran to my apartment to shower.

A difficult interlude in my new neighborhood. No way to be kind or even humane. She must have seen the disgust and fear on my face as I struggled to overcome my revulsion to touch her.

I asked myself, "Who is she?" She is my new neighbor. Will I see her again?

My gratitude to the angel is immense. He was not repelled, as I was. He was not concerned for himself, as I was. He saved us both.

# BARBARA SAPIENZA

**Barbara Sapienza** is the author of the novels, *Anchor Out* and *The Laundress,* which received a starred review from Kirkus. A retired clinical psychologist, she allows her love of people to guide both her life and writing. Barbara practices meditation, tai chi, and dance, and volunteers at Bayside Elementary School in Sausalito where she lives with her husband and watches her grandchildren grow into unique and beautiful flowers. She's currently at work on a novel, *The Dream Being* and a memoir, *Sweet Tears.*

# YELLOW CURRY AND PINK BROMELIADS

Barbara Sapienza

I'm sixty. I have cancer. I have scabies, too. My husband brought it home from a patient he examined. All in the same day these annoyances. Outside my home a pink bromeliad my daughter gave me on Mother's Day feasts on life while cancer eats my scarred, tattooed, etched, sacred, human, radiated body.

In the waiting area of the radiation cathedral at the University of California women write in the communal diary, "God is good." They, my teachers, write of their faith, "God will not give you more than you can take." I read all their beautiful comments. While the bromeliad drenched in the rain of the night accepts her fate, I cannot.

Who is God? I remember my first catechism lesson in a little book. I was seven. Did it have a bleeding sacred heart in thorns on the cover? I don't remember. It's the words that fly into view.

Who made you? God made you.

Who is God? God is a supreme being.

The lesson is not well learned.

It is worn out.

I have dropped the book.

After my treatment I stop at the local Indian restaurant. I look into Basi's deep black eyes. He sees me. "You look good." He says.

"Thank you." I say.

"Don't worry, God will help you," he says.

I bow to him in thanks, "You are God." I say. Tears bubble up from the eternal spring. The vapor from the cardamom—-fennel spiced chai steams up my face meeting my bubbling wells.

Balbir, his wife, chatters in her Punjabi as she stirs the pot of veggie stew, scooping out one bowl for me. They chatter in the small hot kitchen behind the food counter where they live and work, singing kitchen songs.

They feed me. They feed my soul. A man comes in. He wants a chai. He has no money. "Okay, my friend, here is your chai," Basi says, "it's okay."

The man accepts the gift. "I lost my wallet," he says, "I'll pay you later." He leaves.

I taste God's gifts as the yellow curried-potato, carrot, peas, and squash slither down my throat. Piping hot basmati rice oiled and seeded with cumin come to me. Fires of the

Indian kitchen keep me warm on the coldest day of the year, 17 February 2006. "Don't worry, God will help you." He yells from the kitchen, his sweet stretching sounds of satin flow into the room on red ribbons. Men twirl their yellow curried potatoes on their tined forks to weave the red ribbons. Pulsating voices in wavy rivulets billow in circles of love around the pink- and-blue Punjabi room. They sing an eternal song of suffering and glee. A red heart-drum beats through me, an eternal song of suffering and glee on the coldest day of the year.

Tomorrow I will pass my registration card through a sensor and let myself into the changing chamber where I will take off my upper clothing and put on a hospital gown. I will participate in a woman's ritual like menstruation, menses, childbirth, and menopause. I will tell myself I am a woman warrior as I sit in the small waiting area with up to five women who wait to be called. At times we will communicate silently. On occasion we become familiar. We speak of our skin deterioration, ask how many days left, whether it's the first time or a recurrence. Laryngeal, facial, nasal, throat, breast cancer?

I feel lucky I can still eat yellow curry and see bromeliads feasting on life.

# LEANNE SOWUL

**Leanne Sowul** is an award-winning writer and music teacher. Her writing has appeared in such publications as *Barnstorm Journal, Juxta-Prose Literary Magazine, Hippocampus Magazine, Rappahannock Review, Mothers Always Write,* and *Hudson Valley Magazine.* Leanne is also a social justice educator and an elementary band teacher. Her newsletter, the *Joyful Creative,* educates on the purpose and practice of daily creativity. She lives with her family in New York's Hudson Valley.

# OVER THE RAINBOW

Leanne Sowul

On May 14, 2020, I'm making breakfast for my kids when my phone beeps with a calendar alert. "Fourth Grade Spring Concert," it reads.

I put down the butter knife and glance at the clock. It's just after eight-thirty. If not for the pandemic, I would already be in school, setting up chairs and percussion equipment. As my students came in from the busses, I'd have greeted them with cheerleader-level enthusiasm. "It's concert day, Band Kids!" The kids would high-five me, tell me they're nervous or excited or both, list the family members coming to see them perform that night in their very first concert. Later in the morning, we'd play our in-school performance for the younger grades— our dress rehearsal. I think of the cacophony of music stands scraping the stage floor as fifty kids scramble frantically for their seats; the swoosh of the opening curtain; the reveal of the applauding audience; the anticipatory hush, the moment before I raise my baton. And then we'd breathe together, inhale the same air, exhale our music. Unmasked. Unafraid. Together.

Later that morning, around the time the dress rehearsal would have started, I finish helping my son with his online schoolwork and head downstairs to record my weekly band videos. In the days following the abrupt school closing, our district directed teachers to post asynchronous work for our students; virtual meets are optional, but I've been scheduling them anyway, and most kids come. We had a meet yesterday, and I was so relieved to see their faces as they popped onto my screen— fresh, healthy and eager—that my heart burst as I greeted each of them by name.

But today, I'm only talking to myself. I start by recording tutorials of the songs I'm assigning this week. It's hard to play to the camera, to project passion into a flat, pixilated package. Watching my reflection, it's like I'm both teacher and student, performer and audience. The last recording is the hardest: my Friday Fun Video, which is just me playing a song for the kids that they've chosen through suggestions in our Google Classroom. For the last few weeks, the requests have been predictable: "Star Wars" on trumpet; "We Will Rock You" on trombone; "Ghostbusters" on saxophone. Today, a suggestion from one of my fourth grade flute players gives me pause. "Play "Over the Rainbow," Mrs. Sowul," she writes.

I pick up my flute, press record, and begin to play the song. In my mind's eye, I see Judy Garland walking toward the picket fence, her chin uplifted. Her world is gray, stifled, sunless. She knows that this isn't where she's meant to be. She knows there's a better world out there, one that's out of reach. Tears burn my eyes and thicken my throat, but I can't release them because I have to keep breathing. Inhaling air, exhaling music.

I remember all the high school events that cancer took from me. I missed a whole season of marching band, my sophomore homecoming. I mourned those losses for years. My students are too young to be missing so much. This pandemic has cost them joy, pride, togetherness. It has robbed their youth, as cancer once plundered mine.

It's a struggle to play as I weep, and why do I do it? It's so little, this gift of a song. But I push through, and it is not any kind of strength that drives me, but empathy. An understanding, from my inner child to their living childhood. A lament for their loss.

I reach the end. "If happy little bluebirds fly beyond the rainbow, why, oh why, can't I?" I lower my flute. My tear-filled eyes look back at me through the camera. "I miss you, Band Kids," I say. "We'll be together soon. I promise." When this pandemic is over, that's what I'll find over the rainbow: my kids and I making music. Unmasked. Unafraid. Together.

# WENDY TOWNSEND

**Wendy Townsend** is a lifelong lover of animals and has lived with large lizards since she was eight years old. She's a graduate of the Vermont College MFA Program in Writing for Children and Young Adults. Wendy's book, *The Sundown Rule*, was one of Kirkus's 2011 Best Books for Children, and her novel, *Blue Iguana*, was short-listed for the 2015 Green Earth Book Award. Townsend has recently traveled to Jamaica to write about the Jamaican iguana. She is at work on a memoir called *Half Lizard*.

# THE FROG

Wendy Townsend

When the pandemic really took hold, I'd started working 60-hour weeks protecting reptiles and amphibians on utility construction and repair sites. From 7 a.m. to 6 p.m., April through October, I walked the job sites in my hardhat and day-glow vest with my snake stick, and while I moved animals out of immediate harm's way, I watched the destruction of their habitats.

Since then, my crisis hasn't been about illness, or unemployment, but about keeping faith in my purpose. I'm a writer and I don't know any other way to reach readers about biodiversity loss except through emotions. But I couldn't yell loud enough to be heard through a pandemic. I felt ineffective.

I've written my stories of being at a pond, with frogs and turtles, and meeting lizards in a tropical forest. In these wild places, with these living beings, I find acceptance, and a security that can't be taken away, except by the destruction of the ponds and forests. I've hoped readers would grasp what I'm saying and feel as I do about protecting the earth.

Science shows how over-consumption of nature causes pandemics, but I couldn't see social or political will to change our behavior. I wanted to stop striving, and stay home in the barn with my lizards, and write light-hearted things. Then one day, I met a frog on a job site.

My task was to make sure no rare turtles were in the pools of water they were about to drop wooden mats on. I squatted by one and saw no turtles. But there was so much life. Spring peeper and wood frog tadpoles swam through the crisscrossing weed stems with clusters of toad eggs clinging loosely; a dragonfly nymph crawled up one stem, hunting mosquito larvae that wriggled near the water's surface. Another movement caught my eye –a big frog, down in the mud, and then I saw the truck coming.

The truck was a giant, roaring machine attached to a flatbed stacked with wooden mats like huge pallets. Frantically, I felt around in the mud for the frog while the truck drove through the open gate. The diesel engine vibrated in my bones and the tadpoles darted here and there in short, straight lines as though panicked. The truck stopped, its engine rumbling. The driver got out of the cab, walked around back, climbed into a seat, and waited to operate an iron claw on a cable.

Since no rare turtles were present, I had to give the okay. The claw picked up a mat by a chain wrapped around the middle planks and lifted it up in the air, tilting, balancing. Then it swung the huge mat over the pool and dropped it, sending muddy water up in the air and rolling back into the wetland, bending cattails, collapsing, and tearing apart the spider webs between their stalks.

I kept walking the job site, pushing away the image of the frog under the wooden mat, checking other pools for turtles. Later, I walked back. Approaching the pool, I saw the heavy mat covering more than half of it, but then, I also saw a pair of round eyes and a nose above the water's surface—the frog. Relief spread through me, and hope, because there he was, saying, I'm still here!

He dove under when I came close, and I stood looking at the swirl in the water. I saw things a little better, less dire. The world was still in trouble, but I realized that I wanted to keep writing.

On breaks sitting in my truck, a sleepless night in a motel, a Sunday afternoon at home, I pulled together an essay about the frog, and the snakes and turtles on the job sites that was accepted by an on-line magazine.

Writing the essay kept me from giving up on my purpose. It is about the frog's resilience, and mine.

# FRAN TUNNO

**Fran Tunno** is a freelance writer, copywriter, award-winning blogger, voice actress, and mom who, after decades living in Los Angeles, has returned to her Pittsburgh roots. She's truly grateful for the time this pandemic has given her—time to finally finish writing the book she started thirty-five years ago about her hunter-gatherer Italian upbringing in western Pennsylvania in the swinging sixties.

# GRATEFUL FOR COVID?

Fran Tunno

The day I got the phone call from my bosses telling me I was furloughed, I cried. Then I finished writing the commercials I'd been assigned and tried thinking of it as a vacation. I wasn't laid off, just furloughed. Surely our country would rebound once we knocked Covid out.

Then March turned to April, May, June, and in July, I was furloughed for another three months. By then I was running out of Netflix shows and started re-working a children's book I had hopes for.

Chatting with a friend at that time, she said, "Why aren't you finishing that book you wrote about your mom all those years ago?"

I'd re-written that book so many times over the past thirty years, with my ex-husband's words on repeat in my head, "No one's going to want to read your little stories." I hadn't even considered reviving it…until that moment. It was another goal

I regretted not achieving in what I saw as a less than stellar career.

But I'd gotten one of the book's chapters published (which my ex did applaud – I'll give him that) so I thought…I should finish this.

Once I started, I couldn't stop. I finally had time to give my book the meticulous attention and love it deserved. I thought, I'm sixty-five years old, if not now, when?

I felt guilty being grateful for a pandemic when so many people were suffering, but I knew I'd never finish it as long as I had a full-time job. I have a great work ethic for my job and motherhood; unfortunately, my dreams have always taken a back seat.

But my kids couldn't visit. I couldn't serve Sunday dinners. And I had no one to bake for, so tucked away in my apartment with my only daily mandate, a long walk, I kept making progress.

Every day as I worked on my book, I understood my parents and their relationship a little better. I began looking at my mom as an equal because I'm now her age. I finally got her "What the hell" attitude and felt like her spirit was guiding my fingers as I typed.

I pulled out old photos, laughed and cried. I called my brothers and sister and reminisced. I called cousins and learned things I never knew. I relived the exuberance and ugliness of the sixties: the assassinations, the Beatles, the music and the civil rights marches. Watching the news in the summer of 2020 felt like one step forward, two steps back.

But I was also reliving a great childhood filled with delicious homemade ravioli bathed in tomato sauce, meats so tender they fell from the bone, delicious pizza on thick crust with pepperoni and melted mozzarella, and a garden full of fresh vegetables and fruit.

I revisited my embarrassment watching my Italian mom picking dandelions and mushrooms in our front yard, proving to the world in the swinging sixties that we were hunter-gatherers, and were clearly so poor we had to eat weeds.

My first editor gave detailed, insightful feedback, so I rewrote and added fifty pages. Then I sent it to another editor for further review. I rewrote again, adding a few more pages, and now I'm sending it to a third.

Covid ended up striking my family, making my son, my two brothers, and numerous family friends ill. Thankfully, everyone survived and the world seems a bit calmer now. I did lose my job in October, but hopefully I'll get another one, plus an agent and a publisher.

But even if I don't, I enjoyed the most wonderful summer, baking with my mother, gardening with my father, popping sweet grapes in my mouth under the grape arbor, and confronting my biggest fear—that my ex might be right. But I moved forward anyway, finally giving my book and myself permission to soar.

## SUSAN ZELOUF

American writer, furniture designer, and voice artist **Susan Zelouf** lived and worked in New York, Rome and Los Angeles before settling in Ireland with her husband and two Rottweilers. A columnist for The Gloss Magazine (published monthly with The Irish Times) she's written sixty-five columns and a variety of feature pieces to date, riffing on disparate topics from curious to kind, luminous to lost, and messy to modern. Zelouf & Bell's museum-quality furniture is in private collections, public offices, embassy residences, museums, and churches worldwide. In her spare time, Ms. Zelouf is working on assembling a capsule wardrobe.

# THINGS MATTER

Susann Zelouf

A Tuscan friend who works in an agricultural cooperative supplying local farmers with feed and grain (an essential service in locked-down Italy) spends his time off nurturing his family's olive grove. The oil he produces in small batches is intensely green and herbaceous, with notes of arugula, almond, and wild chicory; elegantly bitter, spicy—practically an aphrodisiac when drizzled over creamy white burrata and sweet cherry tomatoes on the vine.

He describes the labor-intensive process of pruning an olive tree as physically draining and emotionally exhausting, with each cut requiring careful consideration, the ramifications of a lopped branch hugely significant for the tree's health and fruit yield. Before the virus, this was shared work, punctuated by gatherings at long tables with food and wine, wives and children, neighbors, babies, and dogs.

Alone, faced with this Herculean task, he wept.

While locked in with her young family in rural County Carlow, unable to access her Dublin studio, an artist friend wondered what she might do to be more useful during the months ahead. Her work tells intimate stories of Ireland's landscape, embedding lustrous hand-cast resins with found objects and collected organic materials such as wildflowers, thistles, mosses, lichens, grasses, seaweeds and shells, delicate and fragile, encased, preserved and contextualised...but, with attention turned towards PPE, vaccines and ventilators, she questioned when, if ever, collectors might consider beautiful things necessary again.

Ireland's beautykeepers—its makers, designers and artisans, alone in their studios, at the bench, the easel, the sewing machine, the lathe, the wheel, the forge, the drawing board—wonder how to go on making in an upside-down world. All of us find ourselves at sea, tasked with redrawing the map; not to pinpoint buried treasure, but to determine what is truly worth having.

And so, from the confines of our cottage in the rural midlands of Ireland, we keep ourselves safe as we watch, in awe, the brave ones at risk. After Earth, a badly reviewed 2013 sci-fi movie directed by M. Night Shyamalan and written by actor Will Smith, redeems itself with a Pinterest-worthy inspirational quote. Printed out and taped to the bathroom mirror, it helps keep the night at bay: "Danger is very real, but fear is a choice." We listen to worried friends— creatives questioning whether their practices will survive, searching for new ways to work,

110

choosing to be more curious than fearful. In response, we consider how we might deepen our commitment to supporting them by surrounding ourselves with meaningful things, ensouled by the hand of the maker.

Lengthy stay-at-home orders encourage intimacy, whether we like it or not; interior landscapes have replaced long haul destinations, the terra incognita are secrets we've been keeping from others, perhaps even from ourselves. Go there. Keeping each other at arm's length finds us more focused on family and friends, our living spaces, walls and wardrobes, our balconies and backyards. We call, we cull, paint, plant, tidy up. Cocooning promises transformation, as if, at the end of isolation, the cocooned emerge as butterflies, with painted rice paper wings.

Writer Robert MacFarlane chose cairn as a word of the day during the pandemic, (from the Gaelic càrn), a stone-stack that acts as path marker, a guide indicating the way forward during bad weather, when the route is uncertain and the going tough. More than just an encroachment of boulders, it means there are those who've preceded us, once lost themselves, and, having managed to find their way, made a conscious decision to leave something meaningful behind. My husband finds an abandoned nest wedged between the thorny branches of a hawthorn (a fairy tree) in the back field. Setting money aside, we commission our friend to cast the nest in resin, part of her ongoing caliology series, "each nest unique to its maker and environment," a testament, a sign, a memento mori.

## EDWARD McCANN
Read650 Founder

**Edward McCann** is an award-winning writer/producer and the Founder and Editor of Read650, celebrating the spoken word with live and digital events in New York City and elsewhere. A regular feature writer for *Milieu* and a longtime contributing editor to *Country Living*, Ed's features and essays have been published in many literary journals, anthologies, and national magazines. He lives and writes in New York's Hudson River Valley.

# ACKNOWLEDGMENTS

In addition to the contributors to this volume—and all the writers who submitted their work for consideration—I'm grateful to Carnegie Hall's Adriaan Fuchs for inviting Read650 to become a presentation partner in the "Voices of Hope" festival. **CarnegieHall.org**

For their help in curating this volume, thanks to Read650 editors Steven Lewis, David Masello, Karen Dukess, and Lisa Donati Mayer.

My sincere thanks to expert copyeditor and thorough fact-checker Shelley Sadler Kenney. Shelley does so much more than cross the t's and dot the i's. **SSKenney@optonline.net**

I'm especially grateful to Sara Caldwell of Convey Media for her help with many technical aspects of Read650's operations, from uploads to downloads and everything in between. **ConveyMedia.com**

For her essential and continued advice, guidance and support, I'm thankful to nonprofits consultant and strategist Susan Ragusa. **SusanJRagusa.com**

Finally, my sincere appreciaton to all you donors who believe and invest in Read650's mission to promote writers. Your generous contributions make everything we do possible, and we simply can't do it without you. Thank you. **Read650.org/donate**

# READ650.ORG

Info@Read650.org
facebook.com/Read650

Made in the USA
Coppell, TX
18 April 2021

53832451R00075